BEST BIBLE STORIES

Danger on the Lonely Road

BEST BIBLE STORIES

DANGER ON THE LONELY ROAD

Jennifer Rees Larcombe
Illustrated by Steve Björkman

CROSSWAY BOOKS • WHEATON, ILLINOIS
A DIVISION OF GOOD NEWS PUBLISHERS

Danger on the Lonely Road

Text copyright © 1992, 1999 by Jennifer Rees Larcombe

Illustrations copyright © 1999 by Steve Björkman

U. S. edition published 2000 by Crossway Books

a division of Good News Publishers

1300 Crescent Street

Wheaton, Illinois 60187

First British edition published 1992

by Marshall Pickering as part of *Children's Bible Story Book.*

This book published as a separate edition in 1999

by Marshall Pickering, an Imprint of HarperCollins Religious,

part of HarperCollins Publishers,

77-85 Fulham Palace Road, London W6 8JB.

Cover design: Cindy Kiple

First U. S. printing 2000

Printed in Hong Kong

ISBN 1-58134-149-0

15 14 13 12 11 10 09 08 07 06 05 04 03 02 01 00

15 14 13 12 11 10 9 8 7 6 5 4 3 2 1

DANGER ON THE LONELY ROAD

Luke 10:25-37

"Go find out what Jesus is

telling people now," the Pharisee told his friends.
"But don't be fooled like others who think that
He's the Messiah!"

But his friends were a
bit curious.

When they got near Jesus, they stopped
and really listened to what
was being said.

"Teacher, how can I have **eternal** life?" asked a man hoping to trick Jesus with a difficult question.
"What does the law say?" replied Jesus.
"It says that we must love God with all of our **heart** and love our neighbors as much as we love ourselves," the expert in the law answered.
"That's exactly right," said Jesus.
But the man, who thought he was a good person, asked, "But who is my **neighbor?**"

"I'll tell you a story that will answer that," said Jesus as everyone gathered closer around Him.

"Once a man was traveling alone from Jerusalem to Jericho."

"**Agh!**" gasped the crowd. They all knew what a lonely, dangerous road that was. It wound between towering rocks, where robbers lurked in the dark shadows, waiting to pounce. Everyone hated to be **alone** on that road.

"Suddenly," continued Jesus, "out jumped a gang of thieves armed with sticks and knives. They stole his money, beat him cruelly and ran away, leaving him bleeding on the ground.

Not long afterwards a priest walked by on his way back from the temple in Jerusalem.

'Tsk, tsk,' he said when he saw the man lying there covered in blood and flies.

'Poor man. But if I stop to help,

I'll spoil my temple clothes.'

So he hurried on past.

The injured man lay **praying** for someone to come. At last he heard footsteps, and around the corner came a Levite. 'He spends his life helping in God's temple,' the man thought.

'Surely he'll help.'

Nervously the Levite crept over and peered down at the wounded man. 'Suppose the robbers who attacked this man are still hiding here,' he shivered.

'They'll probably hurt me too and steal my money.' So off he went and disappeared into the distance.
'No one will come now,' thought the man. 'It's beginning to get dark and by morning I'll be dead.'

It was then that he heard the *clop, clop*

of a donkey's hooves, but his heart sank when he opened his eyes.

'Only a Samaritan. He certainly won't help,' thought the man.

(The Samaritans and the Jews were such enemies, they wouldn't even speak to each other.)

How astonished he was when he felt **kind** hands lifting his head. Someone was giving him a drink and rubbing soothing medicine into his painful cuts.

Strong arms lifted him onto a donkey and took him all the way to a hotel.

'Why is this Samaritan being so kind?' he wondered when he found himself lying in a clean, comfortable bed.

'They stole all my money,' he managed to say.

'Don't worry,'

smiled the Samaritan.
'You can stay here until
you're better;

I'm paying the

bill for you.'"

Jesus looked around at the crowd.

"Which man in that story really loved the injured man?" He asked. "Was it the good Jewish men who always kept the rules?" "No," said the expert in the law uncomfortably.

"It was the Samaritan."

"Then you go and
love
people like that too,"

said Jesus.

"So what did He say?" demanded the Pharisee when his friends came back after seeing Jesus.

Looking very **embarrassed**, his friends replied,

"He told us how to have eternal life—and we're going back to listen to Him more."

Let's talk about the story

1. Why did the expert in the law ask Jesus questions?

2. Who did the expert think were his neighbors? Was he right?

3. Who stopped to help the injured man? Why were people surprised that he stopped to help the Jew?.

4. Who did Jesus teach that our neighbors are?

5. Is there somebody you know that other kids ignore who you could show God's love to? What is one thing you could do to show God's love?